CENGAGE Learning

# Novels for Students, Volume 32

**Project Editor:** Sara Constantakis **Rights Acquisition and Management:** Beth Beaufore, Leitha Etheridge-Sims, Jackie Jones, Kelly Quin **Composition:** Evi Abou-El-Seoud **Manufacturing:** Drew Kalasky

**Imaging:** John Watkins

**Product Design:** Pamela A. E. Galbreath, Jennifer Wahi **Content Conversion:** Katrina Coach **Product Manager:** Meggin Condino © 2010 Gale, Cengage Learning

For product information and technology assistance, contact us at **Gale Customer Support, 1-800-877-4253.**

For permission to use material from this text or product, submit all requests online at **www.cengage.com/permissions.**

Further permissions questions can be emailed to **permissionrequest@cengage.com** While every effort has been made to ensure the reliability of the information presented in this publication, Gale, a part of Cengage Learning, does not guarantee the accuracy of the data contained herein. Gale accepts no payment for listing; and inclusion in the publication of any organization, agency, institution, publication, service, or individual does not imply endorsement of the editors or publisher. Errors brought to the attention of the publisher and verified to the satisfaction of the publisher will be corrected in future editions.

*Gale*
27500 Drake Rd.
Farmington Hills, MI, 48331-3535

ISBN-13: 978-1-4144-4170-2
ISBN-10: 1-4144-4170-3

ISSN 1094-3552

This title is also available as an e-book.
ISBN-13: 978-1-4144-4948-7
ISBN-10: 1-4144-4948-8
Contact your Gale, a part of Cengage Learning sales
representative for ordering information.

Printed in the United States of America
1 2 3 4 5 6 7 14 13 12 11 10

# *The Wings of the Dove*

## Henry James

## 1902

## Introduction

*The Wings of the Dove* by Henry James is a classic story, a simple one, really, in which lovers are victims of the sorrows and inequities of life and are at the same time perpetrators of harm to each other. One of James's later novels, published in 1902, this morality tale is widely acclaimed as his most brilliant work. It is tied to two of his other novels written in the same time period, *The Golden Bowl* (1904) and *The Ambassadors* (1903), which also deal with the psychology of the cruelty of humanity and the struggle to find one's conscience.

This is the love story of Kate Croy and Merton Densher. They are beautiful but poor, although Kate has access to London high society through her Aunt Maud. Into the lives of these characters enters Milly Theale, a young American heiress who is gravely ill. Her naive and innocent presence brings with it the opportunity for charity or for treachery from the worldly and clever Kate and Densher.

The character Milly is based on Minny Temple, James's young cousin to whom he felt an immense attachment. Her death at the young age of twenty-four affected him deeply, and he reveals in his autobiography that the image of her death remained with him for a long time. Her influence on his life and works is seen especially in James's later works; but she appears as early as 1881 as Isabel Archer in *The Portrait of a Lady*.

The language and construction of *The Wings of the Dove* can be difficult to maneuver and some determination and desire is required to understand James's long passages, the ambiguity of his descriptions, and the importance of the silences of his characters in order to know them. The experience of mastering the elusive and rich text is satisfying beyond expectation.

# Author Biography

Henry James was born on April 15, 1843, on Washington Place in New York City to Mary Robertson Walsh James and Henry James, Sr. His father was from a wealthy family and was a noted intellectual and theologian who was well known among the most influential writers and philosophers of the time. The Jameses had five children whom they tutored in several languages and in literature.

After attending Harvard Law School for a short time when he was nineteen, the young Henry realized that he was better suited for writing than for studying law. He published his first short story, "A Tragedy of Error," in 1864 and also became a writer for the literary magazine the *Atlantic Monthly*. His first novel, *Watch and Ward*, was published as a serial in the magazine in 1871 and in book form in 1878.

James moved to Europe in 1875, and his book *Roderick Hudson* was published the next year in 1876. It is the story of a struggling American sculptor living in Rome. *Transatlantic Sketches*, a rendering of the tales of his travels, was published in 1875. *The American*, completed in 1877 while James was living in Paris, deals with the struggles of an American millionaire who is navigating relations with an arrogant, aristocratic French family in Paris. These books constitute the early phase of his career.

Feeling himself ever an outsider, James decided he would never be anything but a foreigner in France and moved back to London in 1878. There he wrote *Daisy Miller* (1879) and *The Europeans* (1878), continuing his theme of contrasting the American spirit with rigid European society. *The Portrait of a Lady* and *Washington Square* were both published in 1881.

James continued to write prolifically during the middle portion of his career. He received great acclaim for *The Portrait of a Lady* at the age of thirty-eight, but critics felt his next offerings, *The Princess Casamassima* and *The Bostonians*, both published in 1886, did not meet their expectations. When *The Tragic Muse* met with little acclaim in 1889, James was bereft of both muse and money. He persevered, and with *What Maisie Knew* in 1897, the short story "The Turn of the Screw" in 1898, and *The Awkward Age* in 1899, he began to reposition himself in the marketplace.

The later years of James's life are his most important in literary terms. These produced his three greatest novels: *The Wings of the Dove* in 1902, *The Ambassadors* in 1903, and *The Golden Bowl* in 1904. He paid a visit to the United States after completing his last novel but found his native country greatly changed. In 1907 he published *The American Scene* that spoke of the troublesome images he had seen in America. Industrialism had taken over, and his despair at America's pollution, ruination, and greed echoed in these essays.

James became a British subject in 1915, but he

is regarded as one of the most prolific and influential American writers. He died in London in 1916.

# Plot Summary

## Book One: Chapters 1-2

In *The Wings of the Dove*, two young London lovers, Kate Croy and Merton Densher, are engaged to be married. Beautiful and resilient, Kate faces poor prospects. Her father has squandered the family money allotted to her mother, who is now dead. Densher is also poor, handsome, and intelligent. Unfortunately, being poor is the greatest thing a man must overcome in England's Victorian age. Densher makes a modest sum of money as a journalist, and Kate lives as the ward of her mother's sister, Maud Lowder. She insists that Kate must marry well, both socially and materially, not making the same mistake as her poor dead mother. Kate is obliged to do what her aunt prescribes, as it is the wish of her father. He is a miserable, conniving man who will no longer have Kate live with him and sees her opportunity with her aunt as one that must surely benefit him. He implores Kate to slyly persuade Aunt Maud to accept her because the conditions under which she will help her ward are stringent: she must renounce her father in all ways possible.

## Book Two: Chapters 1-2

Aunt Maud remains insistent that Densher is not good enough for Kate, but she turns a blind eye to their encounters around London and on her magnificent estate called Lancaster Gate. She finds Densher quite attractive and seems to enjoy having him about, and she has no objection to the young couple's trysts, although she has forbidden them to marry. She does not object to his person, only to his inferiority as a suitor for Kate.

## *Book Three: Chapters 1-2*

The story quickly moves its focus to Milly Theale, a young American heiress from New York, who has come to Europe to experience its culture. Her friend Mrs. Susan Stringham, a writer for American society magazines, has decided to join her as an escort, and she arranges for them to visit her old friend Aunt Maud Lowder in London. The truth is that Milly Theale is dying, and although she is determined to keep it a secret, Mrs. Stringham, her traveling companion, quickly reveals it to her friend. It then becomes Aunt Maud's compassionate duty to introduce the ailing American "princess" to the best of London society. She almost immediately becomes the toast of the town, and many parties are arranged to stage her introduction into London society. At this time, Milly becomes acquainted with Lord Mark, who makes frequent appearances at Lancaster Gate. Although he is now without a fortune, his position in society has made him a proper guest at Lancaster Gate. Aunt Maud thinks he would be a perfect husband for Kate.

# Media Adaptations

- *The Wings of the Dove* was adapted as an American/British film by Hossein Amini, and was directed by Iian Softley. It starred Helena Bonham Carter as Kate Croy, Alison Elliot as Milly Theale, Linus Roache as Densher, Charlotte Rampling as Aunt Maud, and Elizabeth McGovern as Mrs. Stringham. It was released by Miramax Films (1997) in the United Kingdom and in 1998 in the United States. The movie is opulent to watch as it clings faithfully to James's descriptions with lavish silk costumes, magnificent hats, rich furniture all buttoned and tasseled, and ornate jewelry. The film is available in DVD and VHS formats.

- *The Wings of the Dove* is available as an abridged audiobook from Naxos Audio Books and is read by William Hope, who has been the captivating voice on dozens of classic audiobooks. The three-CD set was released in 2006.

- *A Walk to Remember* by Nicholas Sparks was adapted into a screenplay by Karen Janszen and released by DiNovi pictures in 2002. It has a PG rating and is appropriate for teens. There are many correlations between this work and *The Wings of the Dove*, including themes of romance, deception, and death.

## Book Four: Chapters 1-3

Mrs. Stringham learns from Aunt Maud that a previous attachment had been formed between Kate and Densher. Milly has become Kate's new confidante, and Aunt Maud wishes to know if she has learned from Kate whether or not the couple are still involved. Mrs. Stringham and Milly delight in their new roles as detectives and decide to visit Kate's sister, Marian, to find out whether or not there is still an attachment between the two. They are dismayed by the mean conditions in which the widowed Marian lives with her children. After

# Book Nine: Chapters 1-4

Densher devotes himself to Milly, and she quickly falls in love with him. They spend their time gaily in the lavish Venetian palace she has rented for their vacation. Densher, tormented by the deception that he and Kate have plotted, develops true feelings of admiration for Milly. She is delighted with his attentions and asks him why he has stayed behind. He first says it is to write a book, but then confesses it is in order to be with her. Milly has had another visit from Lord Mark, this time to lay before her the deception of Kate and Densher. He tells Milly that Densher is in love with Kate and that they are engaged. He also unveils their plot to inherit her money when she is dead. Densher calls on her but she refuses to see him, and Eugenio turns him away.

After three days, Mrs. Stringham visits Densher. She tells him that Milly has taken to her bed and "turned her face to the wall." She pleads with him to come and reassure her that the accusations made by Lord Mark are untrue. The doctor, Sir Luke Strett, comes to see Densher and tells him that Milly is a bit better and that she would like to see him now.

# Book Ten: Chapters 1-6

Back in London, Densher reveals to Kate that his visit with Milly has been short and heartrending. She has only wanted to see him one last time before her death, and he has revealed nothing of his and

Kate's deceptions towards her. Imminently, they learn of her death. "Our dear dove, as Kate had called her, has folded her wings." Aunt Maud laments. Kate can sense Densher's torment and is sure now that he loved Milly. A letter arrives revealing that Milly has left everything to Densher. He is full of remorse and refuses to accept the money. He promises to marry Kate, but it must be without the acceptance of the money. She says she will marry him if he promises that he can love only her and not the memory of Milly. Then things can be as they were before. But he cannot promise that, and she is left to mourn the fact that "We shall never be again as we were!"

## *Lord and Lady Aldersham*

Lord and Lady Aldersham own the grand house that is the site of a garden party held to introduce Milly to London society. Milly sees them as very elegant, but to her they speak meaningless words and act very superficially. In the house hangs the portrait by the Italian Renaissance painter Agnolo Bronzino that Lord Mark says resembles Milly.

## *Marian Condrip*

Marian is Kate's widowed sister who has three small children. Her poor husband has left a very small inheritance and she lives in poverty. She is pictured as vulgar, red, and fat, and her children survive on mere crumbs. Densher describes her house in Chelsea as "ugly almost to the point of the sinister." Her house is cluttered and dirty, and Marian is awash in self-pity. She looks to Kate to "work" Aunt Maud for more financial support, of which she expects to be the recipient. She is content to sit around with her stepsisters and moan about her condition and wait to hear what Kate has done to improve her dire situation.

## *Kate Croy*

James goes to great lengths to describe Kate's beauty. She has lustrous, thick black hair that falls down beside a clear, fair oval face. Outdoors, in the light, her eyes appear blue, but indoors, in the mirror, they are almost black. She is beautiful, not with the aid of adornments, but completely within the presentation of herself and her gracefulness. She is slender and cleverly underdressed to emphasize that great beauty needs no distractions.

Her father's debaucheries have caused the loss of a great inheritance that belonged to her dead mother. Kate is not undone by her circumstances, and unlike her sister, she rises to the challenge of deciding what she should do about them. She visits her father, and without anger, agrees to take care of him. This seemingly unselfish gesture provides an initial view of her as good-natured and high-minded. It conflicts with the apparently malicious actions she takes against Densher and Milly as the novel progresses. James clearly wants the reader to like Kate in spite of her later transgressions, and she simply does what is necessary for the most positive outcome of things. She is generous, also to her sister Marian, and gives a big portion of her small monthly allotment of money to her.

Kate's sense of duty extends to Densher, whom she truly loves. She tells him eagerly in Book Two, "I engage myself to you forever." When her Aunt Maud forbids them to marry, she takes the matter into her own hands and fashions a plan for Kate to marry Lord Mark. If she must be deceptive, so be it. For this reason, she must take skillful care to disguise her motives when necessary. Milly senses a friendship building between herself and Kate.

Her insincerities become more pronounced as the plot unfolds, and they begin with her half-truth compliments toward Milly: "We all adore you." Milly tells her in strict confidence about her illness and Kate promises not to reveal it to anyone. But it becomes the catalyst for her deception, the main ingredient for her plot. She uses her natural charm and grace to cover her duplicity and her exuberant spontaneity to refashion herself to work her plan into any situation that arises. She slips easily out of the potential danger of being discovered alone with Densher at the National Gallery by "making up" to Milly, giving her new friend her complete attention and basically ignoring Densher. Kate takes control of a situation, moves the circumstances around to her advantage, and skillfully rises above suspicion. She is pragmatic, mercenary, independent, and strong-willed.

She is also quite adept at manipulating others to join in her plot. Initially, she tells Densher that he must simply trust her cleverness and that she will take care of everything. When she puts her plan in motion, she gives Densher only a piece of the puzzle. It is evident to her that Milly loves him, and Kate tells him he should begin to show Milly his favor as well. When he is reluctant, she tells him to trust her; there is more, but she will tell him that later. When she does tell all and he is repulsed, she tells him she will hate him if he "spoils" this for her. Finally, she agrees to go to him in his quarters if he will follow her plan. By pressing her will this far, James sets her up as the ultimate victim. She begins to become less exalted in Densher's eyes, he begins to lose respect for her, and at the end, feeling revulsion for what he has done, he despises her.

## *Lionel Croy*

Mr. Croy is Kate and Marian's father. He lives his life in gross poverty and wretchedness. Kate describes his condition as "the failure of fortune and of honour." In a letter to Kate, he lies, telling her that he is sick; when she comes and offers to live with him and care for him, he makes it clear he has no use for her other than his interest in what money she can get for him from her Aunt Maud. He is handsome and genteel in appearance. He must resort to haggling a living from her, and he, like Marian, will wait to see what the result is.

## *Merton Densher*

Densher appears at the beginning of Book Two as a tall, handsome young Englishman; considered a gentleman only in the sense that he is educated, not wealthy. James likes to write about him in the same manner as he does Milly; in indistinct, ambiguous terms James would rather reveal instead what Densher is not suited to achieve. He is too young for politics, too educated for the army, too skeptical for the church, and too sensible for poetry or art. He is vague without appearing weak; idle without looking empty. Because he is a refined young man who writes for the newspaper, it is acceptable for him to amble about the city on his long legs and gaze up with his head held back in his hands in communion with the sky.

He is convinced that he would be a fool to marry any woman who was not clever and independent. When he meets Kate at a party at a gallery, he immediately sees that she is the kind of woman he wants. Unfortunately, their felicity is short lived, and the naive Densher chooses to bow to the manipulations pressed hard on him by Kate and their economic dilemma. As he follows her scheme to his own "damnation," he is tormented, disgusted, and wracked with guilt. He feels trapped in a "circle of petticoats" as he bows to Kate's wishes: make love to Milly, inherit her money upon her death, and then marry Kate, which will be acceptable to Aunt Maud. His job is to be the savior to Milly and give her happiness and a reason to live. Ironically, she saves him, and he feels redeemed by her purity and brilliance. Exonerated by the refusal of her fortune, he gains the fortitude to propose again to Kate, this time under his own terms.

## *Eugenio*

Eugenio is the well-traveled and highly recommended servant hired by Milly Theale to help with accommodations for her travels abroad. He pays great attention to detail in the arrangements he makes for her comfort. He is very dedicated to her, and she feels he is "very dear and very deep—as probably but a swindler finished to the finger-tips," because he has one hand on his heart and the other in her pocketbook. He proves himself constant and cares for her until the end. Eugenio also plays the role of an accuser to Densher. He recognizes that Densher is only interested in Milly's money and makes the decision to show him he knows it with a look that one con man might give another.

## *Aunt Maud Lowder*

A wealthy London socialite, Aunt Maud Lowder is Kate's aunt and guardian. Kate submits herself as a ward to her benefactor only as a last resort and feels that her estate at Lancaster Gate is like a cage. It is quite a gilded cage and James fixes on Aunt Maud the embodiment of the decay of English society. The description of the house is the description of Aunt Maud: tall, rich, and heavy. It abounds in "rare material—precious woods, metals, stuffs, stones." Densher says he has never dreamed of anything "so fringed and scalloped, so buttoned and corded, ... so much gilt and glass, so much satin and plush, so much rosewood and marble and malachite." Kate calls her the "Britannia of the Market Place—Britannia unmistakable." She also describes her as a wonderful lioness in the cage, a great spectacle for show, "majestic, magnificent, high-coloured, all brilliant gloss, perpetual satin." But the whip will remain always in the hand of the lioness, and she does not hesitate to wield it, as she will against Kate and Densher. The lioness uses her cunning persuasiveness when it comes to having her will accomplished by Mrs. Stringham, Milly, and Lord Mark. To Densher, though she is a formidable foe.

She is London in all its devices. She is resolved that a woman of society has but to be beautiful and marry well. How the money or the suitor is gotten is of little consequence; however, the "working" of persons is her central motivating effort. Kate is chosen for her beauty, and therefore, most of Aunt Maud's work is done. She settles upon Lord Mark as the suitor, and although he does not have much money, he does have his title, which is equally valuable.

## Lord Mark

Lord Mark is a member of the nobility, which makes him worthy and estimable in London society in spite of the fact that he is no longer wealthy. His nobility entitles him more respect than impoverished people of a lower class. He does not work in any business; like Aunt Maud, he is about the business of "working" people.

His age is unknown—he was either "a young man who looked old or an old man who looked young." He is bald, and as Milly sees him, "slightly stale." He is very prim in appearance with his pince-nez. He has an air of aristocratic indifference, and Milly's impression is that he is one of those Englishmen who conceal their thoughts as much as they show them.

Lord Mark has the appearance of cleverness,

but Kate and Densher refer to him as "humbugging." Kate says that his grandeur is simply a result of the fact that he has a duke in his family. He is able to make himself respected without any effort simply by virtue of his aristocratic birth.

He uncovers his treacherous insincerity when he asks Milly to marry him under the guise that he will take care of her when he actually wishes merely to take care of her money. After she refuses him, he takes his revenge and reveals Densher and Kate's plan to her. He obviously has no desire or feelings for her, since this revelation ultimately leads to her broken heart and hastened death. Mrs. Stringham and Densher call him "an idiot of idiots."

## *Sir Luke Strett*

Sir Luke Strett is the physician Milly visits in London to find out more about her illness. She likes him immediately, although on her first visit he is only able to see her for ten minutes. He is so attentive in his manner that she has the impression that she will make a new friend, "wonderfully, the most appointed, the most thoroughly adjusted of the whole collection." He lives up to this impression on her second visit when he realizes that she has what must be a deadly condition (James does not reveal what it is) and goes further to find out details of her family and asks who will take care of her. A look passes between them, and then he smiles to let her know that she can count on him as a doctor, friend, and confidant. He tells her she can depend on him "for unlimited interest," and he remains true to this statement, even following the group to Venice to watch over her. He befriends Densher and goes with him to the galleries and churches there. For Densher, who says that Sir Luke's interest in Milly is "supremely beneficent," he provides relief from the "circle of petticoats." The physician and Milly are in a category of character far above the others, who are consumed with selfish pursuits and imagined injuries. Mrs. Stringham calls him an "angel," which completes Milly's first impression, that he may be a friend from "quite another world." He attends her to the end, through the nights, and then brings her body back to London.

## *Mrs. Susan Stringham*

Mrs. Stringham acts as the "fairy godmother" to Milly, the American heiress. She takes on that role when they leave New York to go abroad. She will help Milly forget her troubles and her illness and will be her guide, helping her to live her life to its fullest. She feels that she is capable of knowing Milly better than Milly knows herself, and she will extend to her what she has observed is lacking in the girl: culture. Mrs. Stringham believes she excels at recognizing culture.

She grasps at the opportunity to assist Milly in helping her escape her circumstances. The romance of the notion appeals to her great but so far stifled imagination. The strangeness of Milly's circumstances—rich, but not beautiful, and lacking culture—impel Mrs. Stringham to devote herself to the young girl. As a Boston writer for gossip magazines, she can present opportunities for romance and adventure. Her view of Milly's tragic situation is "to have ... thousands and thousands a year, to have youth and intelligence," but "not have the opportunity to make the most of her liberty (from poverty), and to live life to its fullest, rather in its present circumstances of confinement in New York."

Mrs. Stringham traveled widely in Europe as a child and she feels herself a woman of the world. As she leads Milly to Europe, she is delighted with the grand accommodations Milly's fortune can afford, but at the same time, she detests the grossness of those who have designs on Milly's wealth. Her motives remain unclear and we do not know whether she is genuinely Milly's champion and protector or just another one of the exploiters among the characters.

## *Milly Theale*

Milly is a young American heiress who has recently lost all of her family in New York. She is also stricken with an illness, the nature of which is never revealed, that is certain to kill her. James describes her in ambiguous terms, sometimes beautiful, sometimes "pale" and "haggard"; she is always portrayed through the musings, thoughts, and conversations of the society about her. She becomes an object in the plot rather than taking on a persona, and she is exploited by everyone. James sets her up as a clear symbol of goodness, generosity, compassion, and humble sacrifice. Hers are the wings of the dove, which in the end, "cover them all."

Many beneficent words can describe Milly: she is wonderful, "magnificent," beautiful, brilliant, "heroic," mysterious, "without sin," kind, graceful, adorable, and a "dove." She is James's tragic heroine who wants desperately to live and love, but as tragedy demands, she must be sacrificed.

## *Victorian Values*

The most important comment James wants to make in *The Wings of the Dove* is that Victorian mores (social customs) cause moral failure. This is a theme seen throughout many of his novels as he purports to make the superficiality of Europe's Victorian Age apparent through its materialism, arrogance, and superciliousness. The American is depicted as naive and inexperienced and is usually the object of a parallel theme: the slaughter of the innocent. In this case, it is Milly who is the tragic victim; she is young, frail, doomed, and impressionable.

## *Religion*

Religious themes are prevalent in *The Wings of the Dove*. Like the spiritual dove that she represents, Milly has all the attributes of the biblical fruit of the spirit: love, joy, peace, patience, goodness, and gentleness, faith, humility, and self-control (Galatians 5:22-23). Hell and damnation plague Densher, Sir Luke acts as the "good physician," and Lord Mark has all the shrewdness and sinister qualities of deviltry. Kate, also culpable, is in some ways absolved because she too is a victim of British decadence, simply following what she has been taught by her father and by Aunt Maud. Densher is plagued by guilt and remorse, and in the end, redemption is available to him. He attains it by refusing Milly's money and risking the loss of Kate's love.

## Topics for Further Study

- Watch the film *A Walk to Remember*. Write an essay comparing the modern-day romance/ tragedy with that of *The Wings of the Dove*. Include your opinions on the similarities of the situations of the main characters. How does Jamie resemble Milly Theale? What deceptions come into play in the relationship between Jamie and Landon, and how does that correspond to *The Wings of the Dove*? What are the similar themes addressed by both works? Who is the counterpart to Kate in the movie? How do the obstacles Jamie has to overcome with her father resemble Kate's struggles with Aunt Maud? Does money or social position have an impact on the characters? How are the stories different?

- Read *In the Garden* by Elsie V. Aidinoff, an Amelia Bloomberg Award selection. In this young-adult novel, the story of the Garden of Eden is told from Eve's point of view. Write an essay based on the ideas from the book that argues whether it is the serpent or Eve who is responsible for the "Original Sin." Include in your argument references to deception, serpent-dove imagery, manipulation, biblical allusions, free will, and determination.

- Write and perform a play with an alternate ending to *The Wings of the Dove*. You may start with the scene in Venice in which Lord Mark tells Milly of Kate and Densher's deception. You may end it however you like. The only requirement is that Densher and Kate act with greater compassion and responsibility toward members of society.

- Make a portfolio of sketches you have drawn of Victorian society: costumes, furniture, architecture, examples of advances in industry, medicine, technology, transportation, food, crafts, labor, cities, *etc.* Include at least ten pieces of artwork. As an alternative, collect images from the Internet and create a PowerPoint presentation.

- Make a short video concerning the theme of death and the fragility of life. It may be a documentary about someone you know or have read about, or it may be simply your philosophy about death. Please do not make the video humorous or macabre (gruesome).

- Using a shared blog, communicate with students from different countries concerning the differences and similarities in your cultures. Try to limit the subjects discussed to how they affect you directly, such as school, clothing, goals, money, entertainment, and the freedoms and restrictions you have. Remember to use proper Internet etiquette. Collect twenty to thirty entries and respond to each comment.

# Revenge

A theme of revenge reveals itself in the character of Lord Mark, when he attempts to destroy Densher and Kate's plan by telling Milly of it.

Greed and insincerity abound among those in the London society depicted in the novel; almost everyone is interested in Milly in some way or another only for her money, and they see her as a commodity to be exploited. Aunt Maud is worthy in society and supreme only because she is wealthy. Mrs. Stringham enjoys the felicities of travel at the expense of Milly's fortune. Kate's plot to have Milly's fortune is simply mercenary. Money earned in "trade" as opposed to being the beneficiary of an inherited fortune is also a topic of note; in terms of one's place in Victorian society, the two were not equal. Lord Mark is worthy in the eyes of society because he has a title, regardless of the fact that he has no money. Densher is not good enough for Kate because he is simply employed as a newspaper writer and has had nothing handed down to him. This puts him on a lower social standing, and Aunt Maud only accepts him because he is handsome.

# Death

Death is a theme that appears repeatedly in James's novels, and in *The Wings of the Dove*, it is present as a force to reckon with almost from the beginning, with the appearance of Milly. It is talked about, not talked about, whispered about, guessed at, and speculated on throughout the entire novel. When Milly finally dies, death is pictured as a release from the vulgarity of this world, and remarkably, as Aunt Maud puts it, "Our dear dove then, as Kate calls her, has folded her wonderful wings…. Unless … she has spread them the wider … for a flight, I trust, to some happiness greater."

## *Feminism*

Feminism is a theme widely touched upon in James's novels. In *The Wings of the Dove*, the advancement of anyone in Victorian society is dependent upon money or title. In this regard, we sympathize with Kate's predicament. Her father has squandered away the inheritance she would have had. As a woman, she has no prospect of being able to earn a living. She is the victim of the devices and designs of her rich Aunt Maud. She must have a husband she did not choose, or she must choose poverty and lose her dignity by marrying the man she does love. There is not any opportunity for her to make her own way in life, to support herself, or to make her own choices.

# Style

## *Omniscient Narrative*

James uses the voice of a third-person omniscient narrator (mysterious and god-like, commenting in and out of the character's thoughts) in *The Wings of the Dove*. This narrator must be listened to very attentively if one wants to understand his meaning. The text is filled with long intricate sentences, rambling circumlocutions, and ideas quizzically tossed about in and out of his character's consciousness. The reader gets lost many times, in understanding who is talking about whom, because of an overuse of ambiguous pronouns in preference to naming the character who is being discussed. In spending so much time in the minds of his characters rather than in their conversations, James is a forerunner of the American stream-of-consciousness writers, who provide a window into the morals, hopes, motives, and feelings of a character without the use of action or dialogue. The technique, a rebellion against the formal prose of the Victorian period, had not been used before the late 1800s, and it was not well received at the time of the novel's publication. Many renowned authors were to follow this style and insight well into the twentieth century.

David Minter, in *A Cultural History of the American Novel: From Henry James to William*

*Faulkner*, comments on the different styles of the American writer:

> We see them in the oblique confessions of Willa Cather's Jim Burden and F. Scott Fitzgerald's Nick Carraway; in the self-conscious fluidity of Gertrude Stein's prose and the self-conscious restraint of Ernest Hemingway's; and in the audacity of William Faulkner's, where concealment matches disclosure, mystification matches expression, and evasion matches revelation.

## Characters and Settings

*The Wings of the Dove* is presently considered one of James's greatest works of fiction. If the absent narrator and the deep delving into characters' consciousnesses confuse the reader, James provides us with familiar things: heroes, heroines, tragedy, love, and redemption. Privy to the rich descriptions played in the minds of the characters, we experience London in the gilded Victorian era. Densher's vision of Aunt Maud's estate is a delightful view of its materialistic decadence.

## Symbols, Metaphors, and Imagery

James's use of symbols and imagery is prolific, and the reader need simply choose one page of the extensive text to experience it. The dove (Milly) is the symbol of peace and redemption. Aunt Maud is the symbol of British materialism and greed. Lord Mark is a symbol of the decay of British high society. Metaphors abound as well: Aunt Maud is a lioness, Sir Luke is an angel, Lionel Croy is a sponge, and Marian Condrip is a relic. The images of Milly as a "priestess" in her black clothing, as a Christ figure (Luke 4:5) when she stands on the hill surveying the "kingdoms of the earth," Densher as "damned" and then "saved" provide conclusive use of religious imagery, though some critics have refused to recognize it.

## Advancements in Science, Industry, Culture, and Thought in the Victorian Era

*The Wings of the Dove, The Portrait of a Lady,* and *The Golden Bowl* are regarded as James's three best novels; they were written in his later years, right at the beginning of the twentieth century. He was an American who had been living in Europe for over forty years. This was the later years of the Victorian era, and coincided with the gilded age in America, because it was a time of great wealth and expansion, and the opulence was apparent in the adornment of everything, from vast mansions and estates to the tassels on a shoe in both countries.

The gilded age was also a time of immense expansion in the areas of culture, science, industry, and philosophy. Hazel Hutchison, in *Seeing and Believing: Henry James and the Spiritual World,* says, "The relationship between environment and consciousness was hotly debated at the beginning of the twentieth century, in the work of psychologist Sigmund Freud." She notes that James "turned sixteen in 1859, the year that Darwin published *The Origin of Species.*"

Darwin's theory of evolution, published in 1909, and Freud's books on psychoanalysis, published in 1900 and 1902, contributed to this time of new ideas. Socioeconomic ideas had been challenged as early as 1848 when Karl Marx published *The Communist Manifesto*. Feminist ideas came forth from the pages of Jane Austen to Virginia Woolf. The rights of women gained immense attention, and it appeared that English women would soon gain the right to vote. The Great Exhibition in London in 1851 had proved England the leader of the world in technology, industry, medical, and scientific advances. American industrialization followed the Civil War. In both countries social classes were changing and there was a tearing down of the old hierarchal society and the rise of a middle class.

---

# Compare & Contrast

- **1902:** Young women in Victorian England usually have arranged marriages. Suitable matches are men who have the same social standing and equal or greater amounts of wealth. Men may choose their own wives but are expected to marry within their own social circles.

  **Today:** An English woman may marry whomever she wishes, but it is still frowned upon if a person of nobility marries a commoner.

- **1902:** English Victorian women are unable to vote.

**Today:** Women are able to vote and play a vital part in British politics, following in the footsteps of Margaret Thatcher, who was England's first female prime minister from 1979 to 1990.

- **1902:** Marriage is the only career for women. They must be attentive to their husbands and never create a scandal. They are unable to obtain profitable or prestigious jobs.

  **Today:** Women can aspire to the highest positions in England in business, in government, and in academia. There is a consensus, even among English businessmen, that there are not enough women in the boardroom.

- **1902:** The very poor are simply ignored by English society. The belief is that people deserve their poverty because they have made bad choices.

  **Today:** Views about poverty have changed dramatically, and a more compassionate effort is practiced in helping the poor in England. The overtures of Princess Diana towards the poor worldwide is remembered as heroic, and one of the best examples of charity work in recent times.

- **1902:** People of the English middle class with a respectable profession can mingle with those of the upper class if the proper introduction is arranged. The only difference between the middle class and upper class is the amount of wealth that has been gained.

  **Today:** Strict class distinctions in England are no longer in place, except for the nobility. Money, however, is still the great equalizer.

# *Money and Greed in the Victorian Era*

*The Rule of Money: Gender, Class, and Exchange Economics*, by Peggy McCormack, shows the importance of money as status in the Victorian Era as depicted in James's works. "Both *The Ambassadors* and *The Wings of the Dove* are pivotal in terms of the protagonist's discovery and efforts to rework the economic exchange systems into which they enter." His characters, with the best intentions, then, are usually innocent, naive Americans. This is exactly the case with Milly Theale, who is the heroine, the sinless dove. But she must go abroad, as directed by Mrs. Stringham, to obtain what she lacks: culture. She must go to

Europe to experience life and cultured civilization. If James sets up England as the ideal culture, he also portrays it as the experienced, shrewd, and knowledgeable society. This creates an immediate conflict between the naive and the experienced, which is used keenly in *The Wings of the Dove*. It depends primarily on what James saw among many in British society: civilization as the art of acquiring all, especially money. To him, deception and corruption must follow. Milly falls victim to this deception and it becomes her demise. Because of Aunt Maud's wealth and social standing, she is free to arrange the lives of others who are less fortunate. Lord Mark represents the decaying of the British social hierarchy. He no longer has money, but his title still affords him a high place in society although it becomes a more pitiable one. With a distinct middle class arising in the Victorian period, a person in his situation historically must lose some regard. Kate also falls victim to the system; as a Victorian woman, she has no way to make her own money.

# Critical Overview

At the time he wrote *The Wings of the Dove*, James had received great acclaim for only two of his novels, *Daisy Miller* and *The Portrait of a Lady*. After a lifetime of producing novels, short stories, plays, and literary criticism, James began to feel distanced from his readers as his novels took on a more difficult style. Critics complained that he walked around and about his characters, never getting to the point, rambling in cumbersome prose, and unintelligible what-ifs.

Judith Woolf, in *Henry James: The Major Novels*, reveals that "the initial stumbling block with Henry James, for many of his readers, is not so much the fact that his novels are complex and oblique and idiosyncratic as a suspicious feeling that such complexity is willful and unnecessary." He began to feel the disconnection, and instead of trying to correct it, as an appeasement, he almost reveled in what he felt was a new freedom. In *The Rule of Money: Gender, Class, and Exchange Economics in the Fiction of Henry James*, Peggy McCormack explains that James spent five years in relative seclusion, out of the public view, to produce his most critically acclaimed novels. From 1899 to 1904, the happy consequence of his therapeutic withdrawal to Lamb House manifested itself in the phenomenal publications of this major phase: *The Sacred Fount, The Wings of the Dove, The Ambassadors, The Golden Bowl*, and *The American*

*Scene.*

In her book *The Critical Reception of Henry James: Creating a Master*, Linda Simon, discussing an essay by H. G. Dwight that appeared in *Putnam's Review* in 1907, writes:

> James was ahead of his time, and Dwight looked forward to a later generation more familiar with fiction that attended to the inner life of characters, more willing to validate a novelist whose interest was not plot but 'in relating the scene of every day to the background of mystery against which it moves.'

Simon goes on to quote Dwight, saying,

> If there is anything at all in what we vaguely called the *Zeitgeist* [the spirit of the times] … it would seem that as consciousness increases, as we become more trained to the consequence of much that we have regarded as inconsequent, books like *What Maisie Knew* and *The Sacred Fount* and *The Golden Bowl* will take on for us a new significance.

This proved to be the case as James's works began to regain popularity in the 1940s, and his influence became evident in the writings of James Joyce and Virginia Woolf, and ultimately he became the forerunner of artists of the stream-of-consciousness style, such as D. H. Lawrence,

William Faulkner, and Ernest Hemingway.

# What Do I Read Next?

- *November Blues*, published in 2007, is a Coretta Scott King Award Honor book by Sharon M. Draper, who also wrote the 2007 Coretta Scott King Literature Award winner *Copper Sun*. It iswritten for young-adult readers but deals with many of the same issues James did concerning deception, guilt, and death.

- *The Portrait of a Lady*, Henry James's 1909 novel, has a heroine who is a wealthy American, much like Milly Theale. Isabel Archer is also enticed to marry the friend of her companion, Merle, who is having an affair with the man. This novel ends differently, though, as Isabel actually marries Merle's lover, Gilbert. Even after she discovers their amour, she remains faithful to her husband.

- *Sister of my Heart* (2000), by Chitra Banerjee Divakaruni, is the story of a young girl from Calcutta who is unable to marry the boy she loves because he is considered unsuitable. A national best seller, it is an enchanting story of love and courage in women bound by mystical cultural beliefs.

- In Elsie V. Aidinoff's *The Garden* (2004), God introduces Eve to the Serpent and he "knows not what he does." An Amelia Bloomer Book Award winner, Aidinoff portrays the Serpent's deception, Eve's act of freeing the world, and the consequences that ensue.

- *Atonement*, by Ian McEwan, published by Doubleday in 2006, exudes the luxury and romance of James's fiction and is imbued with captivating scenes of innocence lost, deception, lies, and tragedy.

- Nicholas Sparks's *A Walk to Remember* (1999) is another tragic novel about young lovers. It includes the issues of societal barriers and the interferences of guardians, a concern throughout *The Wings of the Dove*.

# Sources

Berland, Alwyn, "The Related Ideas," in *Culture and Conduct in the Novels of Henry James*, Cambridge University Press, 1981, pp. 39-40.

Hutchison, Hazel, "The Vain Appearance: Vision and *The Ambassadors*," in *Seeing and Believing: Henry James and the Spiritual World*, Palgrave MacMillan, 2006, p. 81.

————, "The Sacred Hush: Death, Elegy, and *The Wings of the Dove*," in *Seeing and Believing: Henry James and the Spiritual World*, Palgrave MacMillan, 2006, pp. 107-12.

James, Henry, *The Wings of the Dove*, edited by Peter Brooks, Oxford University Press, 1984.

King, Kristin, "Ethereal Milly Theale in *The Wings of the Dove*: The Transparent Heart of James's Opaque Style," in *Henry James Review*, Vol. 21, No. 1, Winter 2000, pp. 1-13.

*Life Application Study Bible: The New Living Translation*, 2nd ed., Tyndale House Publishers, 2004.

McCormack, Peggy, "Exchange Economics after the Major Phase," in *The Rule of Money: Gender, Class, and Exchange Economics in the Fiction of Henry James*, UMI Research Press, 1990, pp. 95, 100.

Minter, David L., "A Dream City, Lyric Years, A

Great War," in *A Cultural History of the American Novel: Henry James to William Faulkner*, Cambridge University Press, 1994, pp. 10-11.

Simon, Linda, "A Mirror for Americans: Contemporary Criticism, 1866-1916," in *The Critical Reception of Henry James: Creating a Master*, Camden House, 2007, p. 24.

Woolf, Judith, Introduction to *Henry James: The Major Novels*, Cambridge University Press, 1991, p 1.

# Further Reading

Faulkner, William, *The Sound and the Fury: the Corrected Text*, Vintage International, 1991.

> The fiction of William Faulkner, amid-twentieth-century writer, is lauded as being among the greatest in American literature. Henry James was a nineteenth-century forerunner of Faulkner's stream of consciousness.

Novick, Sheldon, *Henry James: The Mature Master*, Random House, 2007.

> This biography of Henry James is dedicated to the latter part of his life from 1881 to the end of his life in 1916. This is the period during which he wrote *The Wings of the Dove* and is considered to be the time of his greatest artistic achievement.

Rosenbloom, Robert, and H. W. Janson, *19th Century Art*, Pearson Prentice Hall, 2005.

> This survey of art and sculpture in the nineteenth century is an enormous picture book of over 540 illustrations, 370 of which are in color. It not only gives insight into the culture of James's era, but also

deals with how art was influenced by literature, politics, technology, and music.

Shandley, Mary Lyndon, *Feminism, Marriage, and the Law in Victorian England, 1850-1895*, Princeton University Press, 1993.

This study provides insight into the lives of the Victorian woman and those who sought to change the inequalities of the society. In particular, it discusses the laws concerning marriage, divorce, and married women's property, which at the time gave much greater consideration to men.